Douglas Stankey

PACIFIC LIGHT

IMAGES OF THE MONTEREY PENINSULA

PACIFIC LIGHT

IMAGES OF THE MONTEREY PENINSULA

DOUGLAS STEAKLEY

FOREWORD

BY

JANE SMILEY

POETRY

BY

RIC MASTEN

For information write:

Carmel Publishing Company
P.O. Box 2463
Carmel, California 93921
www.carmeliving.com

Cataloguing-in-Publication Data

Library of Congress Card Catalogue Number: 00 - 106260

Steakley, Douglas

Pacific Light, Images of the Monterey Peninsula

p. cm. ISBN 1-886312-14-1

First Edition

10 9 8 7 6 5 4 3 2 1

Printed in Hong Kong

DEDICATION

To Jackie and Nicole
My wonderful wife and talented daughter.

foreword by Jane Smiley

Some years ago, I took my family to Tuscany, where we stayed in a villa about halfway between Florence and Siena. We did a lot of sightseeing and went to famous restaurants. Our villa had wonderful views from every window, including a view of the Medieval walled town of San Gimignano. The whole time, I was in rather a bad mood, but I didn't put my finger on the reason until almost the end of the trip. What I finally realized was that I was crabby because I couldn't understand why we had gone all the way to Tuscany when we could have stayed on the Monterey Peninsula. Since then, I have repeatedly had something of the same feeling-whatever fabled beauty spot I travel to, I always more or less wonder why I bothered. Almost every fabled beauty spot is less beautiful or less accessible, or more crowded, or more humid, or more polluted than the beauty spots we have all around us between Big Sur and Moss Landing.

The book you hold in your hand, a set of photographs by local photographer Douglas Steakley, with poems by local poet and performance artist Ric Masten, explores much of what there is to see on the Monterey Peninsula, and reminds everyone here, both residents and visitors, why we are privileged to know this place.

First there is the light. As Doug's photographs show, the light all around us here is constantly changing, because the weather is highly variable, both from one minute to the next and from one place ot the next. Many of us who live in Carmel Valley, as I do, have had the experience of leaving home on a summer day in shorts and a t-shirt, and having to buy sweat clothes at the mouth of the Valley–bright hot sunshine has given way to damp fog. Often the weather on the Carmel Valley side of Laureles Grade is different from the weather at the top of the grade, and different again from the weather on the Monterey-Salinas highway. Once, I was in Salinas driving toward the Valley and from a distance I could see fog like a heavy gray blanket nestled along the Carmel River. When I got home, I was told that it had been dark and misty all day-but all the rest of the region, and maybe all the rest of California, had been sunny and hot. Or I have stood at the top of Los Tulares or the top of El Caminito Road, and watched fog drift in like veils over the houses of my friends. Sometimes we gaze out toward Cachagua, and see snow, sometimes we drive toward Carmel and see dark curtains of thunderclouds hanging low, with the sunshine golden and vaporous above them.

Second there is the air, always as crisp and fresh and crystalline as it is possible for air to be at this time in human history. In the Fall of 1999, after a remarkable lightning storm set fires in the Los Padres National Forest, we got an immediate sense of how the air travels on the Peninsula. Those of us living at about mile eight-where Laureles Grade meets Carmel Valley Road–would

Dunes at Seaside Beach

begin to smell the smoke at about four in the morning, as the air cooled and the smoke descended. By the time we were waking up, the odor of the smoke was intense and the Valley lay under a orangey pall. At noon, regular as clockwork, the onshore breezes began to blow, and by three or four, the air was sparkling again. The fires burned for about two months, uncomfortable and expensive, and even apocalyptic in some ways–from parts of the Valley, you could see flames flickering over not so distant ridges–but never enough to drive us away from the air that is otherwise so clean and tingly, as fresh and luxurious as champagne, the air that seems to magnify every view like a lens, and is delicious to all the other senses, as well.

Third, there is the variety of landscape. I have many favorite spots on the Peninsula. If you drive past Stonepine Resort and on past the ranches, some ten miles or so, you will come to a place where the road runs through a narrow valley, and the trees are hung with moss, and the landscape seems as shady and mysterious as anywhere in the American south. If you drive to the top of Los Tulares, and over the ridge, the view from there of the former Berta Ranch is as quiet and peaceful and grand, at all times of the year and all times of day, as some Buddhist monastery somewhere. I love the wide golden ranch lands along Highway Sixty-eight, where cattle graze against the steepness of the mountains. The simple act of driving north up Highway One and

catching sight of Monterey Bay as you breast Carmel Hill is inspiring. Once, a friend of mine flew me in a small plane from the Salinas Valley across the mountains between Arroyo Seco and Carmel Valley Village. The mountains were rough, trackless, and uninhabitable, a sharp reminder of how close we are to the wild here. And, of course, there are the famous places, too-Bixby Bridge, Lover's Point in Pacific Grove, Bird Rock, in Pebble Beach, the list is endless. We do our errands and live our lives everyday in the midst of great natural beauty, both in the largest views and the smallest details, and, for everyone I know, the sense that this is a privilege to be appreciated and cherished never abates.

Fourth, there is the history, gracefully expressed in the differing architectural styles of the different towns-the old adobes of Monterey, the stones of Carmel Mission, the eclectic charm of Carmel-by-the-Sea, the Victorian elegance of Pacific Grove. In all of these towns, the residents have sought to retain the peculiar character of each place, not primarily as tourist attraction, but because each place has a living spirit that the citizens value for itself. If California in general is the land of the new, then the Monterey Peninsula is some other California, the land of many different forms of time: time measured against the tides and the weather and the deep alien darkness of Monterey Bay, time measured against early California history, time measured

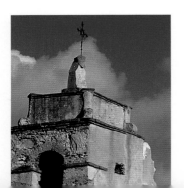

against the wilderness of the national forest and the rocks beneath it, time measured by the short term agricultural calendar of such crops as lettuce and strawberries, and the longer lives of wine grapes and cattle. The Peninsula is neither up-to-date nor behind the times, but rather somewhat apart, special enough so that the normal categories of cultural discourse don't apply.

In this place where special beauty is commonplace, Douglas Steakley's images are remarkable in their ability to single out and body forth things that even the most observant of us rarely catch a glimpse of. These are not just pretty pictures of a pretty place, but an exploration into the unknown dimensions of what is around us. These are not souvenir pictures, but rather true art, where the familiar loses its identity and becomes entirely new and rivetingly powerful. Doug, of course, is of the realist school of photography. His prints are shimmeringly clear, and readily identifiable. He never attempts to trick us or destroy our recognition of the relationship between his subject and the image of it. He is a prowler. He sees some weather or light out the window that might be promising, then goes out and drives around, looking. He takes the natural world on its own terms, but he is remarkably receptive to it and, you might say, he never leaves it alone. These images are the distillation of many drives, many photographs, many prints, many choices. But they don't express hard work, rather it is as if he happened to be exactly in the most splendid spot at the perfect moment when something-a calla lily or a cow or the moon or two or three blossoms against the wall of the Mission-revealed the truest depths of their glory. His pictures seem to show what is always there-he has simply given us the eyes with which to see it. It is this talent for revelation that sets these photos apart from any I have ever seen of our neighborhood.

Often in Doug's photos, the only human presence is the mind behind the camera lens. Ric Masten's poems offer what those of us who live here experience everyday, which is ourselves and those around us. The Monterey Peninsula is thoroughly inhabited. The grandeur around us is filtered through our ideas and moods and varying perceptions. Some of Ric's poems are nostalgic and some are funny; some are appreciative and some are poignant. Throughout, they remind us that it is possible to live in this world and not destroy it, over-run it, reduce it to a parking lot, but to reside right by the beauty, in balance with it.

Doug's images remind us what the camera is for–to catch time in its passing and give ourselves the opportunity to ponder and experience what we would otherwise overlook. They express the unique congruence of a particular place and an individual vision. Each one is a treat. Taken together, they are a wonder.

- Jane Smiley

Photo by Gary Geiger

photographer's note

It's cold–really cold. I'm shaking, my fingers are stiff and I realize I should have brought a pair of gloves–even a light weight pair would help. Now the wind is starting to blow, bringing even more of a chill to the air. Usually the wind doesn't start until later, after the sun has risen and warmed everything. But now it is very early, dark, and I have to wait a little longer for the morning light to turn the sky from pitch black to a royal blue before I can begin taking pictures. Sometimes there is a nice purple cast to the sky that lasts only for a few minutes. I love the magic colors and solitude of daybreak and sunset; the thin light that makes photographs seem mysterious and other worldly.

I think, "This is the coast of California–it shouldn't be this cold." I should know by now that waiting for the sunrise is often uncomfortable–I have done this before. "Next time," I think to myself, "I will pack a heavy down jacket and gloves; ski clothing."

But now the sky begins to lighten and the barn I have been watching slowly emerges from the darkness and begins to turn white. The moon settles lower and is in just the right position. All of a sudden I have to move quickly, make decisions;

vertical or horizontal, what exposure, what f-stop? The exposure time can't be too slow or the moon will blur and it can't be too fast or the picture will be too dark. The well known mechanics of photography become less automatic when I am trembling from the cold and trying to stay warm. The light changes again and I have to react quickly before the scene dissolves. Three quick shots–then I change position and take three more.

The challenge of photographing the Monterey/Big Sur area lies in finding images that are new, fresh, interesting and in some way familiar, but not trite. Often when I drive down Highway 1 toward Big Sur I will pass several serious photographers; they are set up with tripods, taking their time and probably capturing a wonderful scene. This has been going on every day since Edward Weston, Ansel Adams, Wynn Bullock and others discovered this area. I have tried to collect a group of images that are familiar enough for the viewer to recognize from the Central coast area; but different enough to have not been seen many times before.

The idea for this book began several years ago, early one cold morning while I was waiting for the sun to warm the earth and for the colors of the sky to change. I found myself thinking that probably not that many people are interested in leaving their warm bed while it is still dark and cold outside with the hope that there will be an interesting sunrise. I thought I could have something a little different due to my willingness to get up early, or to hike up creek canyons with no trail looking for a waterfall that I had not seen before.

Sometimes getting up before dawn pays off with great images, other times nothing is there and I wonder if sunset shots aren't better anyway. It all depends upon many things, the clouds or fog, the weather and conditions which make the light, which makes the image. Photography is, after all, about the magic of light.

- Douglas Steakley

Tor House, Carmel

poet's preface

what struck me first
was the evidence of an
extraordinarily patient man
imagine the set up
then the sitting down
to wait for light and shadow
to do exactly the right thing
we have here a true believer
certain that he
will be visited by serendipity
and dumb luck

except
for an almost non-existent barn
a distant bridge
the telling mark a highway leaves
this could be Genesis
before the sixth day
Eden without Adam and Eve
but living here
I can assure you life goes on
in and beyond the edge
of these photogenic locations

a scenic photograph is like
the sound of the proverbial tree
falling in the forest
to reverberate
someone must be there
so I've taken the liberty
of populating
these unoccupied spaces
suggesting the invisible
ongoing human presence

think
of the photographs as poems
the words
merely afterthoughts

- Ric Masten

pacific light

the central coast
is lit with what natives call
Pacific light
perhaps because the sun
is born of mountains
and melts into the sea
this subtle variance
seems to effect the landscape
till it looks like nowhere else

try being alone here
spending time
in the space between
the dark before dawn
and the arrival of night
away from all people distractions
allow your self
to ebb and flow with the day
be like the gnomon of a sun dial
throwing a shadow
watching
where and how it creeps
fill albums with what you see

and if what you see
feels vaguely familiar
serene and a bit unreal
trust these feelings
for they are right
that
which colors your imagination
and illuminates your dreams
has always been
closely akin to Pacific light

- Ric Masten

Ribera Beach and Point Lobos

Odello Farm, Carmel

the moon dots

the pre-dawn sky

a period

at the end of a line

describing

Steinbeck country at night

morning is breaking

farms and ranches

will soon be sun lit

and peopled

the long valley

comes to life

Setting moon along River Road, Salinas

Big Sur Coastline

Dawn over Fremont Peak, Carmel Valley

below Fremont Peak

fog blankets the morning

cool and gray

at ground level

the work is laid out

tractors lumber into the field

the workers follow

unaware

that the heavens

are on fire

Point Pinos Lighthouse, Pacific Grove

daybreak has every eye

looking east

at sugar coated foothills

children squealing

surprised by a bank

of white ground clouds

on the Central Coast

natives stare long and hard

at such a temporary sight

knowing that by noon

nothing will remain

but memories

and the proof of it

in a photograph or two

Carmel Valley

a t Point Lobos

mustard blossoms

lie quiet

muted

as morning pushes

the shadow of earth

up the hill

you can see it coming

soon we will be

waist deep

in a riot of yellow

Point Lobos

Mustard flowers at Odello Ranch, Carmel

Fall vineyards along River Road, Salinas Valley

dawn discovers

a crazy quilt of vineyards

spread out along River Road

somewhere else

a toast is being proposed

crystal glasses

clink together

and no one there

knows

that it all started here

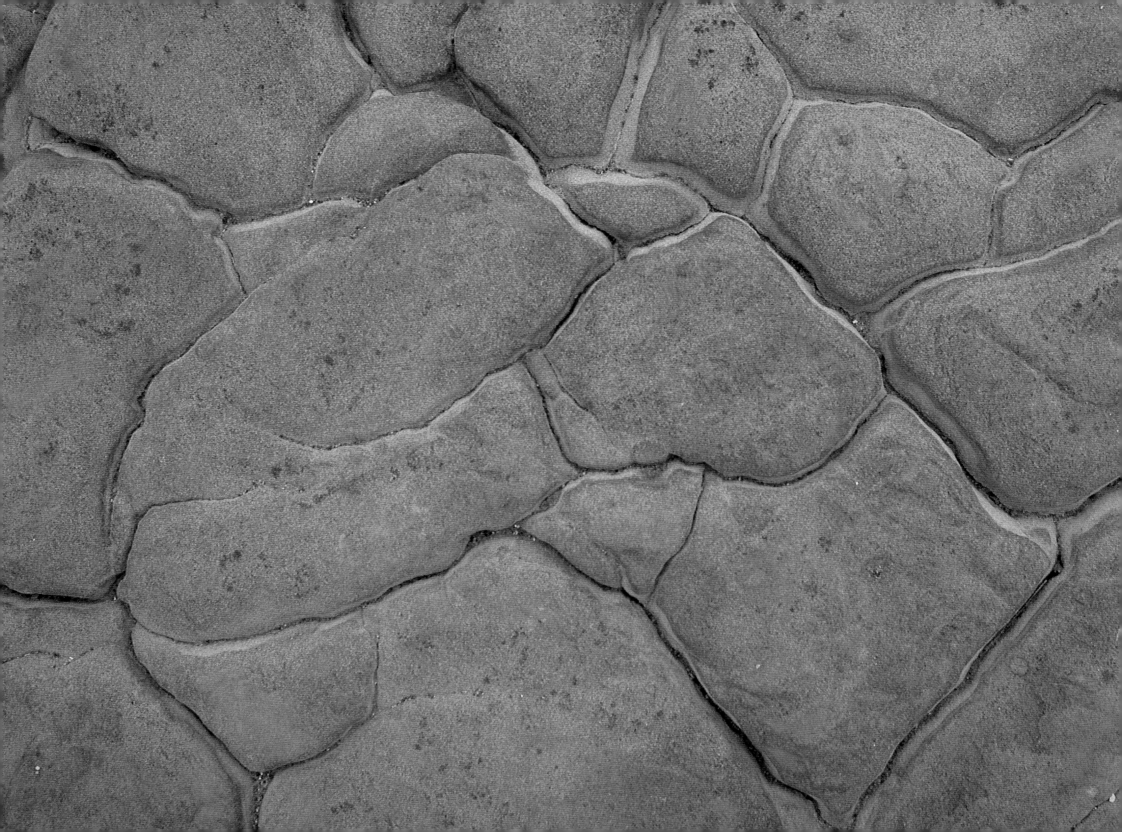

Windswept trees, Point Lobos

Carmel Mission

the Ohlone people

Rumsen and Sargentaruc

are buried here

their descendants

assimilated

in a sense all rubbed out

however

the Native American spirit

still blooms brightly

against

ancient mission adobe

refusing to die

Carmel River at dawn

Pacific Grove

C enturies

of black tail deer

have foraged here

over time

a trail finds itself

meandering at the edge

of sun

and sea washed rock

one cloudy afternoon

I found myself

walking

beside still water

Young elephant seal, Ano Nuevo State Park

i n my childhood

secret passages existed

mystical places where light

came sifting through

the ribbed

gray green canopy

I remember hiding there

motionless

listening to the hum of insects

from far off

someone calls my name

Garland Park, Carmel Valley

Kelp, Carmel Beach

China Cove, Point Lobos State Park

Great Egret, Carmel Valley

Calla lily

you have become

synonymous

with Katherine Hepburn

singular

upright and proper

cup raised…

waiting

for the afternoon rain

to fall

and fill you up

Calla Lily near San Jose Creek, Big Sur

Windswept oak, Carmel Valley

the bearded old man

set in his ways

and deeply rooted

glories in his ability

to defy gravity

he naps this afternoon

the dreamy atmosphere

pregnant

with memories

of rope swings

and picnics

Springtime in Garland Park

Moon over Carmel Valley

Foxglove along Big Sur Coast

Carmel Valley

Redwood bridge along Old Coast Road, Big Sur

a century ago

these redwood trusses

were fresh cut

the planks sharp edged

creaking beneath the weight

of mule drawn carts

hauling out

the lumber and lime

only an echo now

moss covered

and softened by time

Field at Mission Ranch, Carmel

Point Sur Lighthouse

Lightning from Los Laureles Grade

Madrone bark, Carmel Valley

even the trees bend over

to admire their handy work

the atmosphere

of burnished orange

and gold

suggest a royal setting

shades of Autumn

grace Garland Park

bringing Camelot to mind

and Guinevere

out for an afternoon walk

burning with thoughts

of Lancelot

Garland Park trail, Carmel Valley

Pescadero Point, Pebble Beach

China Cove, Point Lobos State Park

long boats have landed here

slipping in on water

so clear

it almost isn't there

pirates and buccaneers

wading ashore

to bury treasure

in Robert Louis Stevenson's

imagination

Carmel Beach

Sunset at Ribera Beach, Carmel

Pico Blanco, Big Sur

Little Sur River

Jeffers knew!

that soaring old predator

sharp eyed... he knew!

if we could speed time up

fast enough

we would see

that the mountains are dancing

and with us

Garrapata Beach, Big Sur

a t high noon

tree trunks bare witness darkly

center stage the sun pools

on a carpet of wood sorrel

enter Ophelia…

barefoot

talking to herself

Canadian geese, Carmel Valley

looking North

from Hurricane Point

I trace the road Kerouac was on

the highway

Brautigan came down

beginning in the late sixties

a generation of flower children

hitch hiked here

colorful pilgrims

making the trek

to Mecca

Oak tree, Carmel Valley

Bixby Bridge from Hurricane Point, Big Sur

Carmel Beach

Kelp at Pfeiffer Beach, Big Sur

We scattered his ashes here

grip loosening slowly

we let him drift

into the foaming wash

onto the coarse wet sand

strangely comforted

at how easily one becomes

part of the beach

part of the whole again

Bixby Creek Beach, Big Sur

Rocky Creek Bridge, Big Sur

this wind swept moor

lacks but two things

the sound of Heathcliff's voice

in the distance

calling out Catherine's name

or closer to home

that outcropping of rock

is the perfect place

for a poet

to strike a craggy pose

eye on the horizon

watching the flight of a hawk

Santa Lucia Preserve, Carmel Valley

Mustard flowers at Odello Ranch, Carmel

California Poppies and lupine, Soberanes State Park, Big Sur

Clearing storm at Palo Corona Ranch, Carmel

Under a sky

heavy with storm

the late afternoon sun

slants in to illuminate

a hillside

spotted with Black Angus

a paved road descends

as graceful as a stroke

of calligraphy

Calla Lily at Soberanes State Park, Big Sur

depending on the size

of the wedding party

at exactly this spot on a trail

in Julia Pfeiffer Burns

the nuptial knot is tied

the bridal veil of McWay Creek

seen falling behind and below

the robed officiant

for years now

lovers have come

to exchange their vows

outdoors

here in God's house

Waterfall at McWay Creek, Big Sur

Asilomar State Beach, Pacific Grove

Carmel Valley

like dinosaurs

a parade of stately old

oak tree stumps

trudge down the slope

concealed in a clump

of blooming lupine

a prehistoric hunter

observes the long shadows

crossing the field below

thinking

this will be a good place

to sleep

hay bales wait

to be loaded in the morning

stacked high on wagons

by strong young men

who laugh and work together

riding on top of the pile

as it is hauled away

in the background

the valley foothills crouch

a pride of lions

passively looking on

Carmel Valley

Cloud reflections, Carmel Beach

legend has it

that while building

Bixby bridge

a worker fell into the forms

becoming encased forever

in one of the giant

concrete piers

I believe this tall tale

but only on evenings

when storm clouds part

and angels

make their presence known

over open water

Clearing storm behind Bixby Bridge, Big Sur

Sunset, Carmel River

Dunes, Seaside Beach

Pfeiffer Beach, Big Sur

Bobcat, Carmel Valley

Waterfall in Garland Park, Carmel Valley

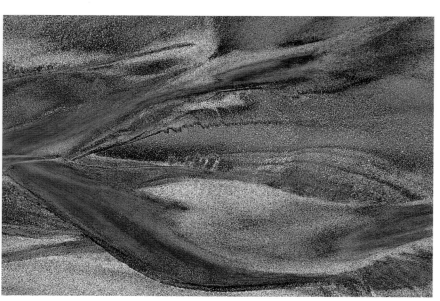

there

are times and places

along this stretch of coast

where everything does

appear other worldly

imagine an astronaut

lost

setting his ship down here

looking around wondering

on what planet

in which galaxy

am I?

Sunset, Pacific Grove

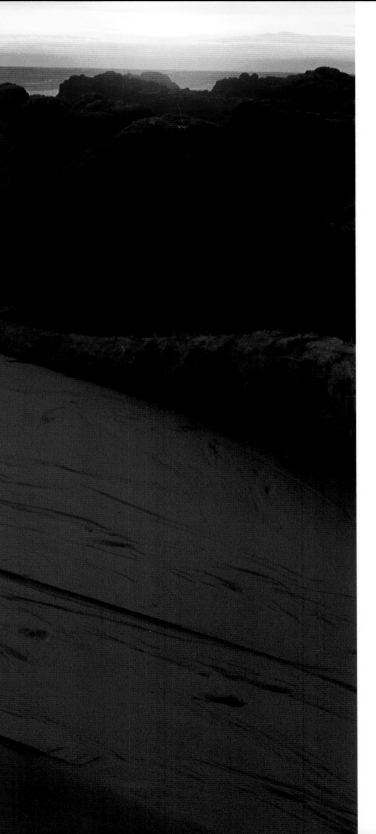

Seasonal creek near Bird Rock, Pebble Beach

like the tip

of ebony icebergs

the rocks surface silently

gleaming

the evening sky

streams across

a plane of reflective sand

all that is needed

to complete this picture

is a set of footprints

made by someone

come to bear witness

Succulent, Point Lobos State Park

Shoreline at Garrapata Beach, Big Sur

even before

the first human being

set foot

on this pristine shore

sunsets

did not go unnoticed

and turning to five

of his spell bound

companions

he exclaimed

"Have you ever seen

anything as glorious

as that?"

Seagulls at Garrapata Beach, Big Sur

Acorns stored in oak tree, Carmel Valley

Carmel Mission

Storm clouds along Big Sur coastline

as mean and devastating

as the storms of El Niño were

they also came ashore

heavily laden

with unimaginable gifts

no doubt

out from under a sky like this

an inspired Michelangelo

came in to begin work

on the ceiling

of the Sistine Chapel

Field along River Road, Salinas

Sunset during fire, Carmel Beach

behind us

the Marble Cone Fire

rages in the Los Padres forest

it darkens the face of August

smoke is everywhere

stopping the sun down

till evening becomes surreal

eyeing the eerie light

that surrounded us

"It looks like

the end of the world!"

we said

saying it

as if we possessed

genetic foresight

Asilomar Beach, Pacific Grove

Ferns in Garland Park, Carmel Valley

Cala Lilies at Garrapata Creek, Big Sur

g arrapata

I've often wondered why

the Spanish chose

to call this lovely stream

and reach of sand "tick"

I suppose

because of the insect

inhabiting the foliage upstream

but forgetting

what the word means

the sound of it

coming off the tongue

is as enchanting as any

sunset seen in Spain

Garrapata Creek at sunset, Big Sur

Lupines and oaks, Carmel Valley

looking for a miracle

they came

from the north and south

to stand separated

dreamers

dreaming of a sky way

a delicate framework

that like a line of poetry

reaches in both directions

and so it was

rarely

do human beings

construct anything

that actually

enhances the sunset

Bixby Creek Bridge, Big Sur

Mustard flowers at Odello Ranch, Carmel

Barns at Odello Ranch, Carmel

naturalists surmise

that the Monterey cypress

migrated from Japan

a thousand years ago

somehow crossing the

Pacific

to take root here

on this barren rocky shore

tonight

against a backdrop of inky

blue

the dark shapely boughs

make even the moon

appear Asian

Rising moon behind cypress tree, Carmel Beach

Monterey Bay

You come

back up the beaches

at the end of day and see

how all your footprints

have been washed away

no

nothing is forever

we are born to die

so may I say "I love you."

before I say "Good-bye."

Ice plant, Pacific Grove

acknowledgements

I am most appreciative to my family—my wife and daughter—for their patience and understanding of the many hours it takes to roam around in search of good photographs. I regret the time we have not been together because I was gone and realize that this time, once lost, can never be recaptured. It is one of the tradeoffs I have chosen, although not without question.

Many photographers have influenced my approach to photography and I would like to thank them all. In particular I would like to acknowledge Galen Rowell. I have taken workshops with Galen, read several of his books and continually read his column in Outdoor Photographer magazine. I appreciate the generosity he displays with his knowledge and techniques, as well as his ability to articulate his thoughts in writing.

I would like to thank Jane Smiley for taking time from her busy schedule to look over these images and write a perceptive and thoughtful Introduction. We have shared interesting and memorable times raising our teenage daughters together.

I also want to thank Ric Masten for his important and meaningful contributions to this book. Ric embraced the idea of writing poems to accompany several of the photographs and fortunately continued to write many more. He is a delightful person to work with in every way.

I appreciate the assistance that I have received from Barbara and Ray March of Carmel Publishing Company. Making a book is a cooperative effort and they have made the process of putting these images together enjoyable and streamlined.

I would also like to thank Tim Sachak and Bunne Hartmann of Hartmann Design Group for their skill, attention to detail and high standards. I have enjoyed our time together producing this book, which has become much more than I originally envisioned due to the contribution of each person who has shared in the process.

Photographs in the book are available in various sizes in limited editions as exhibition prints and are available for stock use. Please contact: Douglas Steakley, P.O. Box 301, Carmel, CA 93921 Tel. 831.624.0661 or www.conceptscarmel.com.

All of the photographs are made from 35mm transparencies taken with Nikon equipment.